AF174177

Conflict
Strategies
INVENTORY   THIRD EDITION

For additional copies of this publication, contact the HRDQ Customer Service Team:

Phone: 610-279-2002

Fax: 610-279-0524

Online: www.hrdq.com

ISBN: 978-1-58854-797-2
Publisher: Martin Delahoussaye
Developers: Eileen M. Russo, PhD, and Matthew P. Eckler
Contributors: Derek T.Y. Mann, PhD, Kate Wartchow, PhD, and Cathy J. Proviano, MEd
Editorial Development: Ashley Thompson and Christina Giampa
Production Editor: Carina Ahren
Graphic Design: T/O Warehouse Creative
Cover image copyright © 2013 by Helder Almeida. Used under license from Shutterstock.com.

 Printed in the United States of America on recycled paper.

0135E3S
EN-03-MY-19

INTRODUCTION

Conflict Strategies Inventory is designed to help you gain a better understanding of the strategies you use in conflict situations. On the following pages, you will find 10 situations that involve different types of conflict that individuals may encounter in their day-to-day work relationships. There are five possible responses provided for each Conflict Situation. The assessment will take about 25 minutes to complete.

INSTRUCTIONS

1 Read each Conflict Situation carefully and consider the five possible responses.

2 Rank the three responses that you would be most likely to use in each situation, assigning points as follows:

> **5 = most likely response**
> **2 = second most likely response**
> **1 = third most likely response**

3 Write these points in the boxes next to the responses.

An example is provided on the next page.

In order to gain the most from the experience, don't view the assessment as a test with "right" or "wrong" answers. The more honest you are with your responses, the more accurate your results will be.

EXAMPLE

You are leading an initiative to make your department more environmentally friendly. However, your supervisor, Eric, has shot down all of your ideas, saying that the excessive cost would far outweigh any advantages. You have done a lot of research and are confident that in the long term, these measures would greatly benefit your department— and ultimately, your organization.

5 = most likely response
2 = second most likely response
1 = third most likely response

A `2` Request a transfer to another department where you might have a more supportive manager.

B `  ` Respect Eric's authority and put your initiative on hold; hopefully, he will change his mind in the future.

C `5` Go to Eric's supervisor and file a complaint that Eric's shortsightedness is getting in the way of a valuable initiative.

D `1` Approach Eric and propose that your department implements several of the less expensive ideas.

E `  ` Set up a one-on-one meeting with Eric to figure out how you can work together to come up with a plan that is both environmentally friendly and cost-effective.

In this example, you chose C as your most likely response (5 points), A as your second most likely response (2 points), and D as your third most likely response (1 point).

Begin the assessment on the next page.

CONFLICT SITUATION #1

Historically, Jim has been in charge of allocating project resources. Because of a long-standing personality conflict between you and Jim, it has become increasingly difficult for you to gain access to certain resources when you need them.

A few months ago, the company hired Alex, an IT specialist, to assist you because of the nature of the projects you work on. Word of Alex's knowledge and expertise has quickly swept through the company, and you are bombarded with unofficial requests for assistance with various computer questions and problems from other people in your division. You have tried to be accommodating to most of the requests, when time permitted, except for the recent requests made by Jim. You view this as your long-awaited revenge for the delays and headaches that Jim has caused you over the years.

Jim has figured out what you are doing, and tensions have greatly increased between the two of you. Alex has told you that she will abide by whatever you decide, but she fears a poor performance rating from the division manager if she does not comply with Jim's service requests. You are finally becoming concerned that something damaging is bound to happen if you and Jim don't resolve this conflict soon.

5 = most likely response
2 = second most likely response
1 = third most likely response

| A | Talk with Jim about this impasse and investigate the sources of this problem to determine ways to eliminate them. You will also suggest that for this discussion an observer be present to minimize any personality blow-ups. |

| B | Approach Jim informally and offer him the same access to the IT specialist as everyone else after a month of his complete cooperation with your requests for project resources. |

| C | Refuse to give in to Jim and make sure that Alex understands that she is *not* to help Jim unless there is an official order to do so from your supervisor. |

| D | Create a sign-up sheet and let Alex fill requests as time permits, in the order that she receives them. |

| E | Tell Alex that from now on *she* should determine whom she helps and when. |

CONFLICT SITUATION #2

When working on division-wide projects, you have had to coordinate your efforts with Danielle, a senior member of another department in your building. Danielle is a more established employee from the sales department. She has many friends and contacts within the organization, and because of this she is given great leeway in what she does.

Whenever it has been necessary to work with Danielle, she has treated your requests as if they were an annoyance. She has told you that she would get to them when/if there was time. This has resulted in missed deadlines, flawed reports, and poor performance reviews for you. Even though you are completing your tasks in a timely and responsible manner, when these projects are mishandled, management places the blame on you.

You just found out that you have been assigned to another division-wide project and will have to interact with Danielle on some crucial aspects of this assignment. You realize that if things go as they have in the past, not only will the project suffer, but there is a good chance that you could lose your job.

5 = most likely response
2 = second most likely response
1 = third most likely response

A   Accept the fact that, in comparison to Danielle, you are at a lower organizational level. You will try to get along with her and do whatever you can to limit the impact that she will have on the final result of this project.

B   Ask your supervisor if it would be possible to work on this project with another person from the sales department so that you might gain more of an understanding about how different people in the division interact with one another.

C   Create a list of tasks and task responsibilities for the aspects of this project that involve a coordinated effort between you and Danielle. Then you will ask Danielle for her input and try to work out a mutually agreeable schedule. The final list will include deadline dates, and a copy of it will be sent to the project manager.

D   Schedule a meeting with the project manager (who supervises all the individuals involved) and present her with examples of how Danielle has hampered your efforts on other projects. You'll tell her that, in order for the upcoming project to be a success, something will have to be done to ensure Danielle's cooperation.

E   Set up a meeting involving just you and Danielle to discuss whether there is anything in the past that you have done that she would prefer you do differently. Then together you will determine what each of you feels the other needs to do in order to complete this project successfully. You'll be open with Danielle about what you are willing to do and what you expect from her.

CONFLICT SITUATION #3

In a recent effort to "trim the fat" in your company, management decided that you and Stephanie, another supervisor in your department, would need to share an administrative assistant. This was made possible by assigning more of the administrative duties back to both of you to handle yourselves. In the beginning, you weren't thrilled with this new way of doing things, but you have since learned how many steps can be eliminated now that you actually have to perform these tasks.

Stephanie has not been receptive to the new system of sharing administrative support. She had the same reservations as you did about the changes, but instead of adapting and working with the new system, she has regressed to the old way of doing things. This has created a logjam with the assistant, and your work is often delayed because of Stephanie's extensive demands. Tension between the two of you has developed, and the assistant is trapped in the middle, not wanting to take sides. You realize that this is affecting the morale in your department and hurting the company.

5 = most likely response
2 = second most likely response
1 = third most likely response

A ☐ Go to your department manager and report Stephanie's blatant disregard for the new policies. You will explain how much it is hurting the company and suggest immediate disciplinary action.

B ☐ Be more friendly in your interactions with Stephanie; hopefully, she will want to do more of her own work in order to maintain the friendship and make things run more smoothly for everyone.

C ☐ Meet with Stephanie and try to determine why she has not accepted the new work arrangement. You plan to share your experiences of how you have successfully made the change to the new system and explore how the new system could be useful to her.

D ☐ Request that you be reassigned so that you can share administrative support with another supervisor with whom you might be more compatible.

E ☐ Tell Stephanie that it is up to her whether or not to abide by the new company policies, but you are instructing the assistant to split her time 50/50 between the two of you.

CONFLICT SITUATION #4

Bill, your supervisor, has been with the organization a long time and has made many friends within the company. He is very autocratic in his ways and does not interact well with visionary types. Your department has lost the chance to work with a couple of very talented and creative individuals because of Bill's strong push to surround himself with disciplined individuals.

Although you are able to handle Bill's style without too much of a problem, Kim, another person in the department, has had more frequent and fiery run-ins with Bill, particularly recently. Because of this you are concerned that Bill may try to get Kim removed from the department. She is very creative and artistic, skills that are hard to come by in your organization, and is a huge asset to your department as well as to the company. You know that Bill has scheduled a meeting at the end of this week with the division manager, at which time he will probably request Kim's removal from the department.

5 = most likely response
2 = second most likely response
1 = third most likely response

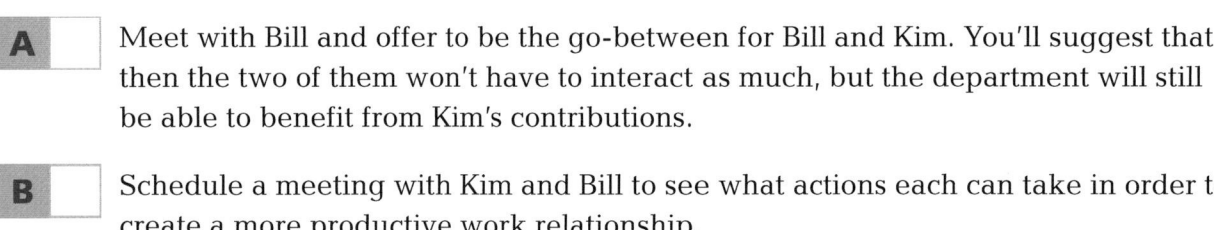

A ☐ Meet with Bill and offer to be the go-between for Bill and Kim. You'll suggest that then the two of them won't have to interact as much, but the department will still be able to benefit from Kim's contributions.

B ☐ Schedule a meeting with Kim and Bill to see what actions each can take in order to create a more productive work relationship.

C ☐ Approach Kim and suggest that she apologize to Bill for her behavior. You'll also tell Kim that you know that she's not wrong, but for now it would be better just to do what Bill wants and not rock the boat.

D ☐ Do nothing, because you fear that if you get involved with this, Bill might decide to terminate you as well.

E ☐ Go to Bill's supervisor and tell him how Bill's bull-headed attitude is going to cost this company a valuable employee. You will insist that something be done to make sure Kim doesn't leave.

CONFLICT SITUATION #5

You and Henry have worked in the same department for a little over six months. Henry is the type of person who will do whatever work is assigned to him, but he rarely takes the initiative to seek out tasks on his own.

Henry's lack of initiative has bothered you, but you have let it go because you felt your supervisor knew who was doing what work, and you felt you were being properly compensated. Recently, however, your company has decided to institute a bonus system to reward high-performing groups. Everyone in your group will receive an equal bonus.

You think this decision is unfair. As far as you are concerned, Henry will be rewarded for your hard work. You've heard Henry say he thinks this system is great. He'll get more money and he doesn't have to work any harder. Because there is no assigned supervisor for each departmental group, the only person you can go to is the manager of your entire department, and you know that she believes strongly in the new reward system.

5 = most likely response
2 = second most likely response
1 = third most likely response

A Sit down with Henry and inform him of your views about his role in the group with regard to the new bonus system. You will ask if you or members of the department can do anything to help in his transition to the equal sharing of responsibility required by the new bonus system. Then together you will try to work out tasks and responsibilities with which he would be comfortable and that would increase his contributions to the group.

B Pull Henry aside and have a one-on-one discussion in which you will tell him that you're not happy with the new bonus system because you feel he hasn't put in the same effort in his job as you have. Then you'll inform him that you are willing to set the past aside, as long as he agrees to become a greater contributor to the group.

C Speak to Henry and tell him that since this new system has been adopted, he had better start being more of a team player and take some initiative, or you'll do everything in your power to get him replaced.

D Accept the new system publicly, do the best job you know how to do, and hope that you will eventually get noticed for doing a superior job.

E Request that you be transferred to another department where you know there is a better shared work effort.

CONFLICT SITUATION #6

You and Larry are old friends. You both started working at this company right out of school and have moved up the ranks at a relatively even rate—you in research and he in marketing. Larry was assigned to work with your department on a four-month project because of a recent downsizing and restructuring of departments. You told your co-workers what a great guy Larry is, and they had looked forward to meeting him.

After two weeks on the project, your co-workers approached you with complaints about Larry. They claimed he was obnoxious, overbearing, and difficult to work with. You assured them that he just comes across a little strong, but deep down he really is a decent person and a hard worker. You have mentioned these complaints to Larry. He feels that your co-workers are uncooperative.

Recently, they approached you again with the same complaints, saying that Larry hasn't changed and in fact he is getting harder to tolerate.

5 = most likely response
2 = second most likely response
1 = third most likely response

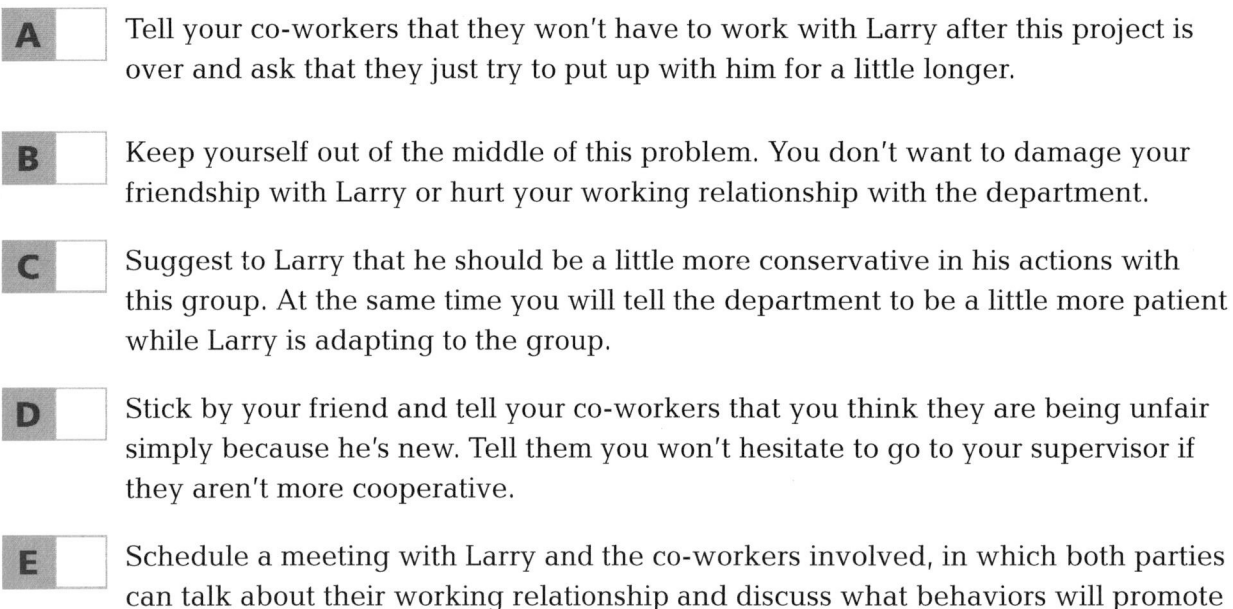

A — Tell your co-workers that they won't have to work with Larry after this project is over and ask that they just try to put up with him for a little longer.

B — Keep yourself out of the middle of this problem. You don't want to damage your friendship with Larry or hurt your working relationship with the department.

C — Suggest to Larry that he should be a little more conservative in his actions with this group. At the same time you will tell the department to be a little more patient while Larry is adapting to the group.

D — Stick by your friend and tell your co-workers that you think they are being unfair simply because he's new. Tell them you won't hesitate to go to your supervisor if they aren't more cooperative.

E — Schedule a meeting with Larry and the co-workers involved, in which both parties can talk about their working relationship and discuss what behaviors will promote more effective interaction among them.

CONFLICT SITUATION #7

Your co-manager, Brian, is a very personable man. Everyone likes him and has a great deal of respect for him. He is, however, a strong believer in following the hierarchical command structure when it comes to decision making. Lately you have fallen behind on certain projects because of the delays incurred waiting for senior management to approve some of the project details.

You have suggested to Brian that together you petition senior management to give you both more control over decisions, which would reduce your downtime while waiting for management approval. Brian is wary of this because he is afraid of making too many decisions with which management might disagree. You are confident in Brian's ability as well as your own to make responsible decisions that would provide a quicker turn-around time for projects. You would rather not offend Brian, but at the same time you strongly believe that the hierarchical system is hurting your productivity.

5 = most likely response
2 = second most likely response
1 = third most likely response

A	Tell Brian straight out that you can't keep functioning in this manner and that sooner or later he will have to accept greater responsibility. You'll suggest that if *he* won't, someone else no doubt will.
B	Accept Brian's preference for how this situation should be handled rather than upset your working relationship.
C	Set up a meeting with Brian and the supervisor to discuss the possibility of both you and Brian having more decision-making responsibility. Then together you'll work out a solution that takes into account Brian's reservations and your desire to keep the project on schedule.
D	Request a transfer to a different project.
E	Ask Brian to agree to letting *you* request a trial period in which you and Brian would be given a chance to demonstrate that you both can handle the responsibility of high-level decision making.

CONFLICT SITUATION #8

Six months ago, you were assigned to lead an organization-wide task force created to design a five-year plan for the company and then take steps to implement it. The task force progressed through its initial stages quite smoothly. The members' personalities were compatible. Motivation was high because almost every member of the task force volunteered for this assignment. But, in your recent project review meeting, you realized that the current goals of the task force were not the same as those that were originally set forth. After some analysis, it was determined that the original goals of the group had been replaced gradually with the individual agendas of certain members.

Assigned roles are now being ignored, and individuals are using the task force as a means of personal gain ahead of the needs of the organization. The project is not far off track, but it will take time to get it back in line with the original mission and goals.

5 = most likely response
2 = second most likely response
1 = third most likely response

A Don't spend the task force's time dealing with the misuse of personal goals. Instead, initiate more checks and balances so that from this point on the mission and goals will be followed more closely.

B Schedule a meeting with the task force and explain that, although you realize that some behavior is bound to occur in self-interest, members must keep the organization's goals ahead of personal ones. Then, together you will determine how members of the task force could be motivated to put their individual needs aside.

C Don't make a big deal about this because in every group situation there will be a few self-serving instances that occur; it's just normal.

D Split up the task force now and reassign the project to a group that will be more focused on organizational concerns.

E Tell the task force that the current situation has to change. Then inform the group that the people who don't put the good of the organization first and their personal needs and views last will not be part of this project much longer.

CONFLICT SITUATION #9

During the course of working on a long-term project with Mary, you and she have overcome the initial difficulties of getting oriented to each other and establishing the basic set-up for the project. Now, however, you face a more difficult dilemma. Confronted with the first real instance of conflict, the two of you cannot seem to agree on the marketing plan for this project. You and Mary each feel strongly about the position the company should take. Mary feels that the company should stay with the traditional, conservative approach that has worked for this type of product for years. You, on the other hand, feel that now is the time to break the old ways of doing things, and this project is the perfect opportunity.

You're concerned that if you don't move past this impasse soon, it will end up delaying the project and perhaps have an irreversible effect on it.

5 = most likely response
2 = second most likely response
1 = third most likely response

A ☐ Have a discussion with Mary to review the original goal of the project. Work together to design a marketing plan that combines the key attributes of both suggestions and that will best serve the company's goals.

B ☐ Suggest to Mary that you try a split marketing plan, targeting some areas conservatively and others more aggressively.

C ☐ Tell Mary that the current situation has to change. You will inform her that if she isn't willing to compromise, you will go to your supervisor and request a new partner for this project who isn't so stuck in the past.

D ☐ Keep going the way that you are, knowing that this type of conflict is normal and will eventually lead to something beneficial.

E ☐ Recognize that you will not be able to work together, split up, and hope that somebody else can take over the project.

CONFLICT SITUATION #10

Your supervisor has just been promoted, and you and Marty, another employee, are competing for the vacant position created by his departure. You and Marty have very different personalities. Marty comes from a sales background, is very outgoing, and likes to make sure everyone knows when he has done something beneficial for the company. You are more introverted. You work hard and do a good job for the company, but you don't like to make a big deal out of your successes.

Marty has been campaigning for this position ever since he got wind that your supervisor might be promoted. He recently has resorted to speaking negatively about you so that he will look better. You really want this promotion and honestly feel that you deserve it more than Marty does. You are furious that Marty is carrying on in this way, but you're not sure what you should do about it.

5 = most likely response
2 = second most likely response
1 = third most likely response

A   Tell Marty that if he gets the promotion, you'll work cooperatively with him. (You hope your gesture will encourage him to stop criticizing you.)

B   Let Marty have the promotion if he wants it badly enough to stoop to this level of behavior.

C   Let Marty know that you're aware of what he's doing, but you're willing to put it behind you if he will stop spreading lies and let management decide fairly who is the best person for the job.

D   Approach Marty and tell him that if he continues with this kind of behavior, you're going to start playing his game. You'll point out that he has a lot more skeletons in his closet than you do in yours.

E   Ask Marty if you and he could talk about what is happening and try to work out any underlying problems the two of you may have. Then you'll determine what might be done so that, whoever becomes the next supervisor, these personal problems won't become the department's problems.

SCORING AND CHARTING THE ASSESSMENT

INSTRUCTIONS

1 Turn to the Scoring Form at the end of this booklet. Carefully tear it out along the perforated line.

2 Refer back to each Conflict Situation. Transfer your assigned points for each response to the corresponding numbered box on the Scoring Form. For example, see below:

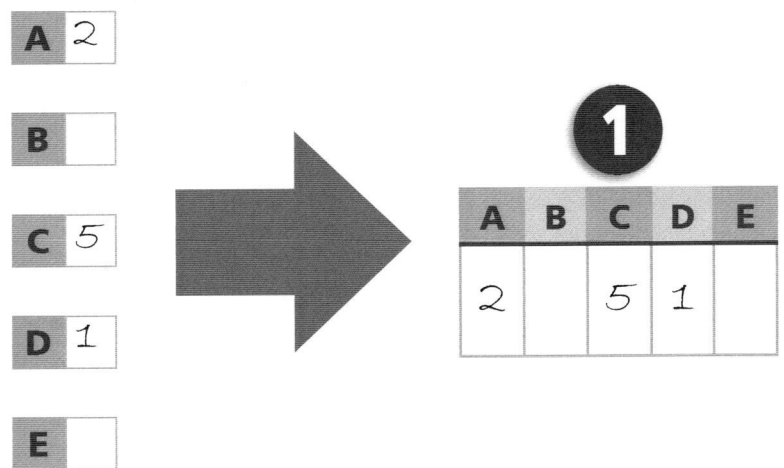

3 Follow the instructions on the Scoring Form to calculate each Strategy Total.

4 Continue by charting your results on the following page.

5 Chart your Strategy Totals on the Conflict Strategies Profile below, which presents the five strategies as columns. Transfer your Strategy Totals from your Scoring Form to the boxes below the columns. Next, draw a bar across each column at the point that represents your Strategy Total, then shade the column up to the bar.

CONFLICT STRATEGIES PROFILE

The diagram below illustrates the degree to which you prefer each conflict strategy.

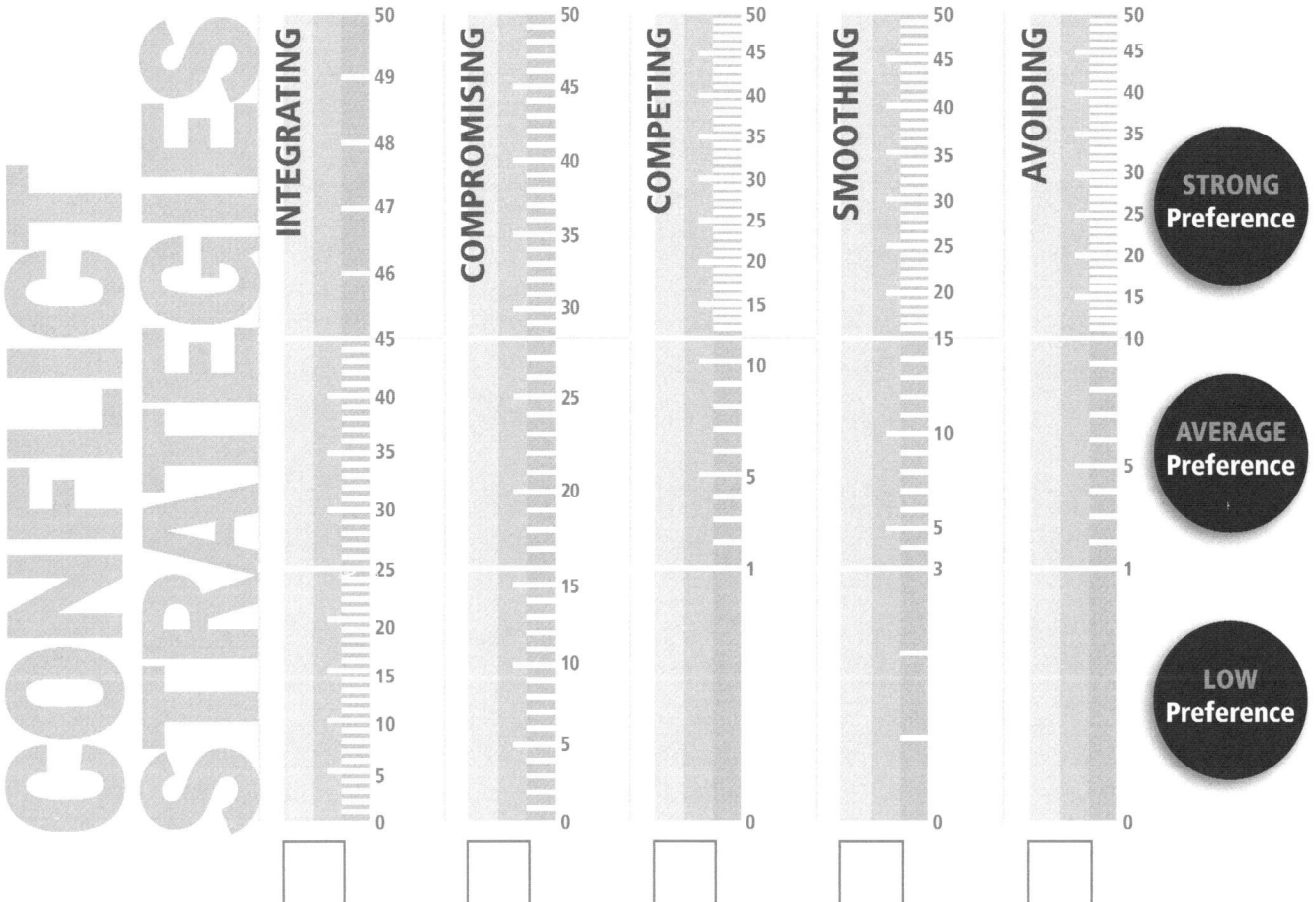

INTERPRETING YOUR RESULTS

On the Conflict Strategies Profile, the conflict strategies are divided into three ranges—Low Preference, Average Preference, and Strong Preference. These ranges are determined by aggregating the scores of others who have taken the *Conflict Strategies Inventory* assessment and calculating the overall average for each strategy. Note that the ranges differ for each strategy. For example, the average for Integrating is 35, while the average for Avoiding is 6. So a score of 20 for Integrating indicates a Low Preference, while the same score for Avoiding indicates a Strong Preference.

Your preferred conflict strategies are the two with the highest bars, not necessarily with the highest numbers. Your primary strategy has the highest bar, and your secondary strategy has the second highest bar. They may fall into the Strong Preference range, the Average Preference range, or a combination of the two.

PREFERRED CONFLICT STRATEGIES

Using your Conflict Strategies Profile for reference, circle your two preferred conflict strategies in the table below. Note which is your primary strategy and which is your secondary strategy.

CONFLICT STRATEGY	CHARACTERIZED BY
INTEGRATING	Goal-oriented solution to conflict; reaching a decision that addresses the concerns of each party; mutually beneficial solution.
COMPROMISING	Reaching an acceptable solution; giving up something to get something else; tradeoffs.
COMPETING	Win-lose mentality; adversarial; standing one's ground; not giving in on issues.
SMOOTHING	Giving in or accommodating the needs of the other party at the expense of one's own needs; going along for the sake of agreement.
AVOIDING	Withdrawing from or sidestepping the conflict; keeping disagreements to oneself; staying away from conflicts entirely.

Focus on your primary and secondary strategies as you read the following descriptions, which will provide you with additional insight into the typical behaviors and effectiveness of each.

INTEGRATING

If you prefer the Integrating strategy, you approach conflict as a problem that is shared by the concerned parties. You generally prefer to work with the other party involved in the conflict to determine the best possible solution—one that is mutually beneficial and addresses the goals of each party. You see conflict as a potential win-win situation. As a result, you probably are gaining the long-term benefits that are possible from conflict resolution.

COMPROMISING

If you prefer the Compromising strategy, you see the benefit of tradeoffs: each party giving up something in order to gain something. You seek an acceptable solution to the conflict, and you may feel that every issue has room for negotiation. You might have a tendency to overstate your goals in a conflict situation so that you will have something to concede. Although you probably are getting some of your needs met, you are not achieving the best possible solution for either party.

COMPETING

If you prefer the Competing strategy, you usually fight for what you want and stand your ground. You probably view conflict as a win-lose situation, and you want to win. You may thrive on competition and be likely to force an issue in order to get your way. Your focus on your own success may cause you to ignore the needs and feelings of the other party involved in the conflict.

SMOOTHING

If you prefer the Smoothing strategy, you frequently put other people's goals ahead of your own. You may gloss over conflict in the interest of maintaining harmony. You might have a strong need to be accepted by your colleagues. This need can translate into giving in when there is a conflict situation. As a result, you may be neglecting your own needs.

AVOIDING

If you prefer the Avoiding strategy, you tend to remove yourself from existing conflict situations and steer clear of those on the horizon. You may dislike the tension that conflict creates. The frequent use of Avoiding may also indicate that you have a tendency to undervalue your contributions to the process of resolving conflict.

SCORING FORM

INSTRUCTIONS

1 Carefully tear out this page along the perforated line.

2 Enter the points that you assigned to each Conflict Situation's responses into the corresponding boxes.

3 Next, add the A scores, B scores, C scores, D scores, and E scores for Conflict Situations 1, 5, and 9. Place the resulting Subtotals in the boxes below (follow the lines down).

4 Repeat this process for the remaining groups of Conflict Situations (3 and 7; 2, 6, and 10; and 4 and 8).

5 Add the Subtotals across each row of boxes and record the resulting Strategy Totals.

6 Turn to page 14 to chart your results.

1 A B C D E

2 A B C D E

3 A B C D E

4 A B C D E

5 A B C D E

6 A B C D E

7 A B C D E

8 A B C D E

9 A B C D E

10 A B C D E

SUBTOTALS

A   C   E   B   **STRATEGY TOTALS** — **INTEGRATING**

B   E   C   A   **COMPROMISING**

C   A   D   E   **COMPETING**

D   B   A   C   **SMOOTHING**

E   D   B   D   **AVOIDING**